*Wilfred Owen*

# The Works of
# Wilfred Owen

**with an Introduction by Douglas Kerr,
and Bibliography**

**Wordsworth Poetry Library**

This edition published 1994 by Wordsworth Editions Ltd,
Cumberland House, Crib Street, Ware, Hertfordshire SG12 9ET.

Copyright © Wordsworth Editions Ltd 1994.

ISBN 1-85326-423-7

Printed and bound in Denmark by Nørhaven.

The paper in this book is produced from pure wood
pulp, without the use of chlorine or any other substance
harmful to the environment. The energy used in its
production consists almost entirely of hydroelectricity
and heat generated from waste materials, thereby
conserving fossil fuels and contributing little to the
greenhouse effect.

# CONTENTS

# INTRODUCTION

AT MIDNIGHT on New Year's Eve, at the end of 1917, Wilfred Owen was writing a letter to his mother, and recalling that exactly a year before he had been at the great military camp at Étaples in France, on his way for the first time to the front line of the war. He remembered listening to the revelling of the Scottish troops, who would soon be dead, and wondering if he himself would survive the year.

> But chiefly I thought of the very strange look on all the faces in that camp; an incomprehensible look, which a man will never see in England, though wars should be in England; nor can it be seen in any battle. But only in Étaples. It was not despair, or terror, it was more terrible than terror, for it was a blindfold look, and without expression, like a dead rabbit's.
>
> It will never be painted, and no actor will ever seize it. And to describe it, I think I must go back and be with them.

This fatal vocation to witness – for Owen did return to the war, and was killed at the age of twenty-five, a week before the fighting ended – is the basis of his reputation as the best-known of the poets of the Great War, and one of the outstanding English writers of modern times. All of Owen's important work in poetry was written in just over a year, the last year of his life, and almost all of its is about the war. 'My subject is War, and the pity of War', he declared. 'The Poetry is in the pity'. But it was not to be simply a poetry of mourning, and still less of consolation. 'All a poet can do today is warn', he went on. 'That is why the true Poets must be truthful'.

It was not the kind of poetry he had envisaged writing, as a youth with his head full of the romantic odes of Keats and Shelley and, a little later, the dark and sensuous thrills of the late-romantic Decadents. But there were, in any case, several good reasons why he should not have become a poet at all. His home circumstances were not very encouraging. His father was vigorous, practical, and unimaginative, his mother a very devout evangelical Christian but poorly educated. He grew up in a religious atmosphere which was suspicious of the arts. There was never enough money, and his parents could not afford to send the children to university. For a long time the young Owen knew very little about the work of modern poets, and had almost no one to talk to about poetry. It was to be only in his last year, with the help of his friend Siegfried Sassoon, that Owen came into contact with other young writers, and all through his short career he had to do his writing in time snatched from other duties and commitments. (Even in the war hospital he was to complain that he only had time to be a poet for a quarter of an hour after breakfast.) He published no book, and only a small handful of his poems appeared in periodicals in his lifetime. Outside a small circle, he was quite unknown when he died.

Wilfred Owen was born in Oswestry in Shropshire in 1893, the eldest child of a family struggling to maintain its foothold in the genteel middle class. Tom Owen's job as an official with a railway company took the family first to Birkenhead and then to Shrewsbury, and Wilfred received good schooling at the Birkenhead Institute and at Shrewsbury Technical School. There was a passionate closeness between Wilfred and his mother – 554 of 673 letters in the *Collected Letters* are addressed to her – and his relations with his father were consequently difficult, though the family as a whole was a tightly-knit and even rather claustrophobic little community. (Wilfred's brother Harold was to write a fascinating chronicle of the Owen family in his *Journey from Obscurity*.) With his father out at work all day his mother frequently ill in bed, Wilfred as a child was used to taking charge of his sister and brothers, in a pattern that oddly anticipated the responsibilities of the junior officer which he would later assume.

In 1911, when he left school, he had a passion for poetry and poets, an enthusiasm for botany and music, good French, a thorough knowledge of the Bible (all factors that would shape his later writing) and no career prospects. At his mother's prompting, he became lay assistant to the vicar of the village parish of Dunsden near Reading. His fifteen months at Dunsden were a formative period. The social work which was an important part of his duties as the vicar's assistant brought him into disturbing contact with the miseries of poverty, illness, and unemployment, and aroused the pity and indignations which were to speak eloquently in his war poems and letters. Meanwhile the vicar's lordly indifference (as Owen saw it) to the sufferings outside his gates was also an anticipation of the callous insensibility of age and authority, which was to become another of Owen's themes.

> But cursed are dullards whom no cannon stuns,
> That they should be as stones...
> By choice they made themselves immune

> To pity and whatever moans in man
> Before the last sea and the hapless stars;
> Whatever mourns when many leave these shores;
> Whatever shares
> The eternal reciprocity of tears.

When he left Dunsden early in 1913, Owen had lost his Christian faith.

His next move took him to Bordeaux, where he found work as a teacher of English, and he had made for himself a busy, independent and happy life in France when the Great War broke out in 1914. It was not until October 1915 that he enlisted as a cadet with the Artists' Rifles in London. After initial training he was commissioned as a second lieutenant in the Manchester Regiment. To his surprise, he enjoyed the disciplines and comradeship of the army. But when eventually he was posted to the front line of battle bear Beaumont Hamel in January 1917, his initiation was brutal. It was like arriving in a frozen hell – 'a sad land, weak with sweats of dearth,/Grey, cratered like the moon with hollow woe,/And pitted with great scabs and pocks of plagues'. War had struck the landscape like a revolting disease. In that deadlocked campaign, the life of the ordinary soldier was a combination of boredom, terror, suffering and hopelessness, a state of destitution which Owen's poems compassionately evoke.

> Bent double, like old beggars under sacks,
> Knock-kneed, coughing like hags, we cursed through sludge,
> Till on the haunting flares we turned our backs
> And towards our distant rest began to trudge.
> Men marched asleep. Many had lost their boots
> But limped on, blood-shod. All went lame, all blind;
> Drunk with fatigue; deaf even to the hoots
> Of tired, outstripped Five-Nines that dropped behind.

But if soldiers were the victims of war, war had also made them killers, and Owen not only depicts their sufferings but also explores painful themes of responsibility and guilt.

> I am the enemy you killed, my friend.
> I knew you in this dark...

There is no self-pity in his poems, but he returns often to his own role as a junior officer, for it was his job to look after his men, but also to lead them into danger and to punish them if they flinched from it. By May 1917 his own nerves had given way. He was labelled 'neurasthenia', and sent to the shellshock hospital at Craiglockhart, outside Edinburgh. It was there that he was befriended by a fellow-patient, the soldier-poet Siegfried Sassoon, who was to give him the encouragement and direction he needed. Sassoon had written satirical and realistic poems about the war, and had been sent to the shellshock hospital after he made a public protest against the continuation of the war. Sassoon's example showed Owen that to tell the truth about the horror of war was not an act of cowardice.

Almost all of Wilfred Owen's war poems were written during his convalescence, and in the months of home service that followed, before he returned to the front at the end of August 1918, two months before his death in battle. His creativity liberated at Craiglockhart by Sassoon's example, he was soon combining a Sassoon-like realism with a romantic lyric poignancy and a visionary mode which derived from Shelley and, beyond him, from Dante. His particular stylistic signature was the consonantal rhyme or pararhyme, the uneasy rhyming which in 'Strange Meeting' pairs *friend* and *frowned,* and *killed* with *cold*. And although Owen's declared subject was 'War, and the pity of War', we can find glimpses of his whole life here – his reading, his homosexuality, his friendships, his love of music, his philosophical doubts and his physical enjoyments. These poems contain all his personal history. 'Futility', for example, a poem that turns accusingly on the generative sun for failing to restore the life of a dead soldier, carries traces of Owen's quarrels with his own father, with the religion whose promises of resurrection he could no longer believe, and with a long-established tradition of poetic elegy that sought self-deluding consolation for the death of loved ones.

> Are limbs, so dear achieved, are sides
> Full-nerved, still warm, too hard to stir?
> Was it for this the clay grew tall?
> – O what made fatuous sunbeams toil
> To break earth's sleep at all?

Owen was not a pacifist, but described himself as 'a conscientious objector with a very seared conscience'. His disgust and compassion, his anger and his courage, have done as much as any other individual to shape the ways we understand and feel about modern war. Consumed with the urgency of his duty to warn, he claimed that above all he was 'not concerned with Poetry'. But if he had not been concerned with poetry we would not remember him, and his warnings would have no chance of being heeded.

The first collection of Owen's poems was edited by his friend Siegfried Sassoon in 1920. The present edition follows the texts established by the scholar and poet Edmund Blunden, himself a former infantry officer and poet of the Great War. A definitive edition, with some important textual revisions and containing more than a hundred and seventy poems and fragments, was edited by Jon Stallworthy and first appeared in 1983.

*Douglas Kerr*
*Oxford, 1994*

## FURTHER READING

Harold Owen, *Journey from Obscurity*, 3 vols, 1963-5.
*Wilfred Owen: Collected Letters*, ed. Harold Owen and John Bell, 1967.
Jon Stallworthy, *Wilfred Owen: A Biography*, 1974.
*The Poems of Wilfred Owen*, ed. Jon Stallworthy, 1983.
Dominic Hibberd, *Owen the Poet*, 1986.
Dominic Hibberd, *Wilfred Owen: The Last Year*, 1992.
Douglas Kerr, *Wilfred Owen's Voices*, 1993.

# POEMS

## BY

# WILFRED OWEN

# FROM MY DIARY, JULY 1914

Leaves
  Murmuring by myriads in the shimmering trees.
Lives
  Wakening with wonder in the Pyrenees.
Birds
  Cheerily chirping in the early day.
Bards
  Singing of summer scything thro' the hay.
Bees
  Shaking the heavy dews from bloom and frond.
Boys
  Bursting the surface of the ebony pond.
Flashes
  Of swimmers carving thro' the sparkling cold.
Fleshes
  Gleaming with wetness to the morning gold.
A mead
  Bordered about with warbling water brooks.
A maid
  Laughing the love-laugh with me; proud of looks.
The heat
  Throbbing between the upland and the peak.
Her heart
  Quivering with passion to my pressed cheek.
Braiding
  Of floating flames across the mountain brow.
Brooding
  Of stillness; and a sighing of the bough.
Stirs
  Of leaflets in the gloom; soft petal-showers;
Stars
  Expanding with the starr'd nocturnal flowers.

# THE UNRETURNING

Suddenly night crushed out the day and hurled
Her remnants over cloud-peaks, thunder-walled.
Then fell a stillness such as harks appalled
When far-gone dead return upon the world.

There watched I for the Dead; but no ghost woke.
Each one whom Life exiled I named and called.
But they were all too far, or dumbed, or thralled;
And never one fared back to me or spoke.

Then peered the indefinite unshapen dawn
With vacant gloaming, sad as half-lit minds,
The weak-limned hour when sick men's sighs are drained.
And while I wondered on their being withdrawn,
Gagged by the smothering wing which none unbinds,
I dreaded even a heaven with doors so chained.

# TO EROS

In that I loved you, Love, I worshipped you,
In that I worshipped well, I sacrificed
All of most worth.  I bound and burnt and slew
Old peaceful lives; frail flowers; firm friends; and Christ.

I slew all falser loves; I slew all true,
That I might nothing love but your truth, Boy.
Fair fame I cast away as bridegrooms do
Their wedding garments in their haste of joy.

But when I fell upon your sandalled feet,
You laughed; you loosed away my lips; you rose.
I heard the singing of your wing's retreat;
Far-flown, I watched you flush the Olympian snows
Beyond my hoping. Starkly I returned
To stare upon the ash of all I burned.

# MY SHY HAND

My shy hand shades a hermitage apart,
O large enough for thee, and thy brief hours.
Life there is sweeter held than in God's heart,
Stiller than in the heavens of hollow flowers.

The wine is gladder there than in gold bowls.
And Time shall not drain thence, nor trouble spill.
Sources between my fingers feed all souls,
Where thou mayest cool thy lips, and draw thy fill.

Five cushions hath my hand, for reveries;
And one deep pillow for thy brow's fatigues;
Langour of June all winterlong, and ease
For ever from the vain untravelled leagues.

Thither your years may gather in from storm,
And Love, that sleepeth there, will keep thee warm.

# STORM

His face was charged with beauty as a cloud
With glimmering lightning. When it shadowed me
I shook, and was uneasy as a tree
That draws the brilliant danger, tremulous, bowed.

So must I tempt that face to loose its lightning.
Great gods, whose beauty is death, will laugh above,
Who made his beauty lovelier than love.
I shall be bright with their unearthly brightening.

And happier were it if my sap consume;
Glorious will shine the opening of my heart;
The land shall freshen that was under gloom;
What matter if all men cry aloud and start,
And women hide bleak faces in their shawl,
At those hilarious thunders of my fall?

*October* 1916.

# MUSIC

I have been urged by earnest violins
And drunk their mellow sorrows to the slake
Of all my sorrows and my thirsting sins.
My heart has beaten for a brave drum's sake.
Huge chords have wrought me mighty: I have hurled
Thuds of God's thunder. And with old winds pondered
Over the curse of this chaotic world,
With low lost winds that maundered as they wandered.

I have been gay with trivial fifes that laugh;
And songs more sweet than possible things are sweet;
And gongs, and oboes. Yet I guessed not half
Life's sympathy till I had made hearts beat,
And touched Love's body into trembling cries,
And blown my love's lips into laughs and sighs.

*October* 1916–1917.

# SHADWELL STAIR

I am the ghost of Shadwell Stair.
  Along the wharves by the water-house,
  And through the dripping slaughter-house,
I am the shadow that walks there.

Yet I have flesh both firm and cool,
  And eyes tumultuous as the gems
  Of moons and lamps in the lapping Thames
When dusk sails wavering down the pool.

Shuddering the purple street-arc burns
  Where I watch always; from the banks
  Dolorously the shipping clanks,
And after me a strange tide turns.

I walk till the stars of London wane
  And dawn creeps up the Shadwell Stair.
  But when the crowing syrens blare
I with another ghost am lain.

# HAPPINESS

Ever again to breathe pure happiness,
The happiness our mother gave us, boys?
To smile at nothings, needing no caress?
Have we not laughed too often since with joys?
Have we not wrought too sick and sorrowful wrongs
For their hands' pardoning? The sun may cleanse,
And time, and starlight. Life will sing sweet songs,
And gods will show us pleasures more than men's.

But the old Happiness is unreturning.
Boy's griefs are not so grievous as youth's yearning,
Boys have no sadness sadder than our hope.
We who have seen the gods' kaleidoscope,
And played with human passions for our toys,
We know men suffer chiefly by their joys.

# EXPOSURE

Our brains ache, in the merciless iced east winds that
    knive us . . .
Wearied we keep awake because the night is silent . . .
Low, drooping flares confuse our memory of the salient . . .
Worried by silence, sentries whisper, curious, nervous,
        But nothing happens.

Watching, we hear the mad gusts tugging on the wire,
Like twitching agonies of men among its brambles.
Northward, incessantly, the flickering gunnery rumbles,
Far off, like a dull rumour of some other war.
        What are we doing here?

The poignant misery of dawn begins to grow . . .
We only know war lasts, rain soaks, and clouds sag stormy.
Dawn massing in the east her melancholy army
Attacks once more in ranks on shivering ranks of gray,
        But nothing happens.

Sudden successive flights of bullets streak the silence.
Less deadly than the air that shudders black with snow,
With sidelong flowing flakes that flock, pause, and renew,
We watch them wandering up and down the wind's
    nonchalance,
        But nothing happens.

Pale flakes with fingering stealth come feeling for our faces—
We cringe in holes, back on forgotten dreams, and stare,
    snow-dazed,
Deep into grassier ditches. So we drowse, sun-dozed,
Littered with blossoms trickling where the blackbird fusses.
        Is it that we are dying?

Slowly our ghosts drag home: glimpsing the sunk fires, glozed
With crusted dark-red jewels; crickets jingle there;
For hours the innocent mice rejoice: the house is theirs;
Shutters and doors, all closed: on us the doors are closed,—
  We turn back to our dying.

Since we believe not otherwise can kind fires burn;
Nor ever suns smile true on child, or field, or fruit.
For God's invincible spring our love is made afraid;
Therefore, not loath, we lie out here; therefore were born,
  For love of God seems dying.

To-night, His frost will fasten on this mud and us,
Shrivelling many hands, puckering foreheads crisp.
The burying-party, picks and shovels in their shaking grasp,
Pause over half-known faces. All their eyes are ice,
  But nothing happens.

# FRAGMENT: "CRAMPED IN THAT FUNNELLED HOLE"

Cramped in that funnelled hole, they watched the dawn
Open a jagged rim around; a yawn
Of death's jaws, which had all but swallowed them
Stuck in the middle of his throat of phlegm.

[And they remembered Hell has many mouths],
They were in one of many mouths of Hell
Not seen of seers in visions; only felt
As teeth of traps; when bones and the dead are smelt
Under the mud where long ago they fell
Mixed with the sour sharp odour of the shell.

# FRAGMENT: "IT IS NOT DEATH"

It is not death
  Without hereafter
To one in dearth
  Of life and its laughter,

Nor the sweet murder
  Dealt slow and even
Unto the martyr
  Smiling at heaven:

It is the smile
  Faint as a [waning] myth,
Faint, and exceeding small
  On a boy's murdered mouth.

# THE PARABLE OF THE OLD MEN
# AND THE YOUNG

So Abram rose, and clave the wood, and went,
And took the fire with him, and a knife.
And as they sojourned both of them together,
Isaac the first-born spake and said, My Father,
Behold the preparations, fire and iron,
But where the lamb for this burnt-offering?
Then Abram bound the youth with belts and straps,
And builded parapets and trenches there,
And stretchèd forth the knife to slay his son.
When lo! an angel called him out of heaven,
Saying, Lay not thy hand upon the lad,
Neither do anything to him. Behold,
A ram, caught in a thicket by its horns;
Offer the Ram of Pride instead of him.
But the old man would not so, but slew his son,
And half the seed of Europe, one by one.

# ARMS AND THE BOY

Let the boy try along this bayonet-blade
How cold steel is, and keen with hunger of blood;
Blue with all malice, like a madman's flash;
And thinly drawn with famishing for flesh.

Lend him to stroke these blind, blunt bullet-heads
Which long to nuzzle in the hearts of lads,
Or give him cartridges of fine zinc teeth,
Sharp with the sharpness of grief and death.

For his teeth seem for laughing round an apple.
There lurk no claws behind his fingers supple;
And God will grow no talons at his heels,
Nor antlers through the thickness of his curls.

# THE SHOW

We have fallen in the dreams the ever-living
Breathe on the tarnished mirror of the world,
And then smooth out with ivory hands and sigh.
                                        W. B. YEATS.

My soul looked down from a vague height with Death,
As unremembering how I rose or why,
And saw a sad land, weak with sweats of dearth,
Gray, cratered like the moon with hollow woe,
And pitted with great pocks and scabs of plagues.

Across its beard, that horror of harsh wire,
There moved thin caterpillars, slowly uncoiled.
It seemed they pushed themselves to be as plugs
Of ditches, where they writhed and shrivelled, killed.

By them had slimy paths been trailed and scraped
Round myriad warts that might be little hills.

From gloom's last dregs these long-strung creatures crept,
And vanished out of dawn down hidden holes.

(And smell came up from those foul openings
As out of mouths, or deep wounds deepening.)

On dithering feet upgathered, more and more,
Brown strings, towards strings of gray, with bristling spines,
All migrants from green fields, intent on mire.

Those that were gray, of more abundant spawns,
Ramped on the rest and ate them and were eaten.

I saw their bitten backs curve, loop, and straighten,
I watched those agonies curl, lift, and flatten.

Whereat, in terror what that sight might mean,
I reeled and shivered earthward like a feather.

And Death fell with me, like a deepening moan.
And He, picking a manner of worm, which half had hid
Its bruises in the earth, but crawled no further,
Showed me its feet, the feet of many men,
And the fresh-severed head of it, my head.

# THE SEND-OFF

Down the close, darkening lanes they sang their way
To the siding-shed,
And lined the train with faces grimly gay.

Their breasts were stuck all white with wreath and spray
As men's are, dead.

Dull porters watched them, and a casual tramp
Stood staring hard,
Sorry to miss them from the upland camp.
Then, unmoved, signals nodded, and a lamp
Winked to the guard.

So secretly, like wrongs hushed-up, they went.
They were not ours:
We never heard to which front these were sent.

Nor there if they yet mock what women meant
Who gave them flowers.

Shall they return to beatings of great bells
In wild train-loads?
A few, a few, too few for drums and yells,
May creep back, silent, to village wells
Up half-known roads.

# GREATER LOVE

Red lips are not so red
  As the stained stones kissed by the English dead.
Kindness of wooed and wooer
Seems shame to their love pure.
O Love, your eyes lose lure
  When I behold eyes blinded in my stead!

Your slender attitude
  Trembles not exquisite like limbs knife-skewed,
Rolling and rolling there
Where God seems not to care;
Till the fierce Love they bear
  Cramps them in death's extreme decrepitude.

Your voice sings not so soft,—
  Though even as wind murmuring through raftered
    loft,—
Your dear voice is not dear,
Gentle, and evening clear,
As theirs whom none now hear,
  Now earth has stopped their piteous mouths that
    coughed.

Heart, you were never hot,
  Nor large, nor full like hearts made great with shot;
And though your hand be pale,
Paler are all which trail
Your cross through flame and hail:
  Weep, you may weep, for you may touch them not.

# INSENSIBILITY

## I

Happy are men who yet before they are killed
Can let their veins run cold.
Whom no compassion fleers
Or makes their feet
Sore on the alleys cobbled with their brothers.
The front line withers,
But they are troops who fade, not flowers
For poets' tearful fooling:
Men, gaps for filling:
Losses who might have fought
Longer; but no one bothers.

## II

And some cease feeling
Even themselves or for themselves.
Dullness best solves
The tease and doubt of shelling,
And Chance's strange arithmetic
Comes simpler than the reckoning of their shilling.
They keep no check on armies' decimation.

## III

Happy are these who lose imagination:
They have enough to carry with ammunition.
Their spirit drags no pack,
Their old wounds save with cold can not more ache.
Having seen all things red,
Their eyes are rid
Of the hurt of the colour of blood for ever.

And terror's first constriction over,
Their hearts remain small-drawn.
Their senses in some scorching cautery of battle
Now long since ironed,
Can laugh among the dying, unconcerned.

### IV

Happy the soldier home, with not a notion
How somewhere, every dawn, some men attack,
And many sighs are drained.
Happy the lad whose mind was never trained:
His days are worth forgetting more than not.
He sings along the march
Which we march taciturn, because of dusk,
The long, forlorn, relentless trend
From larger day to huger night.

### V

We wise, who with a thought besmirch
Blood over all our soul,
How should we see our task
But through his blunt and lashless eyes?
Alive, he is not vital overmuch;
Dying, not mortal overmuch;
Nor sad, nor proud,
Nor curious at all.
He cannot tell
Old men's placidity from his.

### VI

But cursed are dullards whom no cannon stuns,
That they should be as stones;
Wretched are they, and mean
With paucity that never was simplicity.

By choice they made themselves immune
To pity and whatever moans in man
Before the last sea and the hapless stars;
Whatever mourns when many leave these shores;
Whatever shares
The eternal reciprocity of tears.

# DULCE ET DECORUM EST

Bent double, like old beggars under sacks,
Knock-kneed, coughing like hags, we cursed through
      sludge,
Till on the haunting flares we turned our backs,
And towards our distant rest began to trudge.
Men marched asleep. Many had lost their boots,
But limped on, blood-shod. All went lame, all blind;
Drunk with fatigue; deaf even to the hoots
Of gas-shells dropping softly behind.

Gas! GAS! Quick, boys!—An ecstasy of fumbling,
Fitting the clumsy helmets just in time,
But someone still was yelling out and stumbling
And floundering like a man in fire or lime.—
Dim through the misty panes and thick green light,
As under a green sea, I saw him drowning.

In all my dreams before my helpless sight
He plunges at me, guttering, choking, drowning.

If in some smothering dreams, you too could pace
Behind the wagon that we flung him in,
And watch the white eyes writhing in his face,
His hanging face, like a devil's sick of sin;
If you could hear, at every jolt, the blood
Come gargling from the froth-corrupted lungs,
Bitter as the cud
Of vile, incurable sores on innocent tongues,—
My friend, you would not tell with such high zest
To children ardent for some desperate glory,
The old Lie: Dulce et decorum est
Pro patria mori.

# THE DEAD-BEAT

He dropped,—more sullenly than wearily,
Lay stupid like a cod, heavy like meat,
And none of us could kick him to his feet;
Just blinked at my revolver, blearily;
—Didn't appear to know a war was on,
Or see the blasted trench at which he stared.
"I'll do 'em in," he whined. "If this hand's spared,
I'll murder them, I will."

                A low voice said,
"It's Blighty, p'raps, he sees; his pluck's all gone,
Dreaming of all the valiant, that aren't dead:
Bold uncles, smiling ministerially;
Maybe his brave young wife, getting her fun
In some new home, improved materially.
It's not these stiffs have crazed him; nor the Hun.

We sent him down at last, out of the way.
Unwounded;—stout lad, too, before that strafe.
Malingering? Stretcher-bearers winked, "Not half
Next day I heard the Doc.'s well-whiskied laugh:
"That scum you sent last night soon died. Hooray

# THE CHANCES

I mind as 'ow the night afore that show
Us five got talking,—we was in the know,—
"Over the top to-morrer; boys, we're for it.
First wave we are, first ruddy wave; that's tore it."
"Ah well," says Jimmy,—an' 'e's seen some scrappin'—
"There ain't more nor five things as can 'appen;—
Ye get knocked out; else wounded—bad or cushy;
Scuppered; or nowt except yer feeling mushy."

One of us got the knock-out, blown to chops.
T'other was hurt like, losin' both 'is props.
An' one, to use the word of 'ypocrites,
'Ad the misfortoon to be took be Fritz.
Now me, I wasn't scratched, praise God Amighty
(Though next time please I'll thank 'im for a blighty),
But poor young Jim, 'e's livin' an' 'e's not;
'E reckoned 'e'd five chances, an' 'e 'ad;
'E's wounded, killed, and pris'ner, all the lot,
The bloody lot all rolled in one. Jim's mad.

# ASLEEP

Under his helmet, up against his pack,
After the many days of work and waking,
Sleep took him by the brow and laid him back.
And in the happy no-time of his sleeping,
Death took him by the heart. There was a quaking
Of the aborted life within him leaping . . .
Then chest and sleepy arms once more fell slack.
And soon the slow, stray blood came creeping
From the intrusive lead, like ants on track.

 .      .      .      .      .      .

Whether his deeper sleep lie shaded by the shaking
Of great wings, and the thoughts that hung the stars,
High-pillowed on calm pillows of God's making
Above these clouds, these rains, these sleets of lead,
And these winds' scimitars;
—Or whether yet his thin and sodden head
Confuses more and more with the low mould,
His hair being one with the grey grass
And finished fields of autumns that are old . . .
Who knows? Who hopes? Who troubles? Let it pass!
He sleeps. He sleeps less tremulous, less cold,
Than we who must awake, and waking, say Alas!

# S. I. W.

I will to the King,
And offer him consolation in his trouble,
For that man there has set his teeth to die,
And being one that hates obedience,
Discipline, and orderliness of life,
I cannot mourn him.
                                    W. B. YEATS.

## I. THE PROLOGUE

Patting good-bye, doubtless they told the lad
He'd always show the Hun a brave man's face;
Father would sooner him dead than in disgrace,—
Was proud to see him going, ay, and glad.
Perhaps his mother whimpered; how she'd fret
Until he got a nice safe wound to nurse.
Sisters would wish girls too could shoot, charge, curse;
Brothers—would send his favourite cigarette.
Each week, month after month, they wrote the same,
Thinking him sheltered in some Y.M. Hut,
Because he said so, writing on his butt
Where once an hour a bullet missed its aim
And misses teased the hunger of his brain.
His eyes grew old with wincing, and his hand
Reckless with ague. Courage leaked, as sand
From the best sand-bags after years of rain.
But never leave, wound, fever, trench-foot, shock,
Untrapped the wretch. And death seemed still withheld
For torture of lying machinally shelled,
At the pleasure of this world's Powers who'd run amok.

He'd seen men shoot their hands, on night patrol.
Their people never knew. Yet they were vile.

"Death sooner than dishonour, that's the style!"
So Father said.

## II. THE ACTION

One dawn, our wire patrol
Carried him. This time, Death had not missed.
We could do nothing but wipe his bleeding cough.
Could it be accident?—Rifles go off . . .
Not sniped? No. (Later they found the English ball.)

## III. THE POEM

It was the reasoned crisis of his soul
Against more days of inescapable thrall,
Against infrangibly wired and blind trench wall
Curtained with fire, roofed in with creeping fire,
Slow grazing fire, that would not burn him whole
But kept him for death's promises and scoff
And life's half-promising, and both their riling.

## IV. THE EPILOGUE

With him they buried the muzzle his teeth had kissed,
And truthfully wrote the Mother, "Tim died smiling".

# MENTAL CASES

Who are these? Why sit they here in twilight?
Wherefore rock they, purgatorial shadows,
Drooping tongues from jaws that slob their relish,
Baring teeth that leer like skulls' teeth wicked?
Stroke on stroke of pain,—but what slow panic,
Gouged these chasms round their fretted sockets?
Ever from their hair and through their hands' palms
Misery swelters. Surely we have perished
Sleeping, and walk hell; but who these hellish?

—These are men whose minds the Dead have ravished.
Memory fingers in their hair of murders,
Multitudinous murders they once witnessed.
Wading sloughs of flesh these helpless wander,
Treading blood from lungs that had loved laughter.
Always they must see these things and hear them,
Batter of guns and shatter of flying muscles,
Carnage incomparable, and human squander,
Rucked too thick for these men's extrication.

Therefore still their eyeballs shrink tormented
Back into their brains, because on their sense
Sunlight seems a blood-smear; night comes blood-black;
Dawn breaks open like a wound that bleeds afresh.
—Thus their heads wear this hilarious, hideous,
Awful falseness of set-smiling corpses.
—Thus their hands are plucking at each other;
Picking at the rope-knouts of their scourging;
Snatching after us who smote them, brother,
Pawing us who dealt them war and madness.

# FUTILITY

Move him into the sun—
Gently its touch awoke him once,
At home, whispering of fields unsown.
Always it woke him, even in France,
Until this morning and this snow.
If anything might rouse him now
The kind old sun will know.

Think how it wakes the seeds,—
Woke, once, the clays of a cold star.
Are limbs, so dear-achieved, are sides,
Full-nerved—still warm—too hard to stir?
Was it for this the clay grew tall?
—O what made fatuous sunbeams toil
To break earth's sleep at all?

# CONSCIOUS

His fingers wake, and flutter; up the bed.
His eyes come open with a pull of will,
Helped by the yellow May-flowers by his head.
The blind-cord drawls across the window-sill . . .
What a smooth floor the ward has! What a rug!
Who is that talking somewhere out of sight?
Why are they laughing? What's inside that jug?
"Nurse! Doctor!" "Yes; all right, all right."

But sudden evening muddles all the air—
There seems no time to want a drink of water,
Nurse looks so far away. And everywhere
Music and roses burnt through crimson slaughter.
He can't remember where he saw blue sky.
More blankets. Cold. He's cold. And yet so hot.
And there's no light to see the voices by;
There is no time to ask—he knows not what.

# DISABLED

He sat in a wheeled chair, waiting for dark,
And shivered in his ghastly suit of grey,
Legless, sewn short at elbow. Through the park
Voices of boys rang saddening like a hymn,
Voices of play and pleasures after day,
Till gathering sleep had mothered them from him.

   ·    ·    ·    ·    ·    ·

About this time Town used to swing so gay
When glow-lamps budded in the light blue trees,
And girls glanced lovelier as the air grew dim,—
In the old times, before he threw away his knees.
Now he will never feel again how slim
Girls' waists are, or how warm their subtle hands;
All of them touch him like some queer disease.

   ·    ·    ·    ·    ·    ·

There was an artist silly for his face,
For it was younger than his youth, last year.
Now, he is old; his back will never brace;
He's lost his colour very far from here,
Poured it down shell-holes till the veins ran dry,
And half his lifetime lapsed in the hot race,
And leap of purple spurted from his thigh.

   ·    ·    ·    ·    ·

One time he liked a blood-smear down his leg,
After the matches, carried shoulder-high.
It was after football, when he'd drunk a peg,
He thought he'd better join.—He wonders why.
Someone had said he'd look a god in kilts,
That's why; and may be, too, to please his Meg;
Aye, that was it, to please the giddy jilts
He asked to join. He didn't have to beg;

Smiling they wrote his lie; aged nineteen years.
Germans he scarcely thought of; all their guilt,
And Austria's, did not move him. And no fears
Of Fear came yet. He thought of jewelled hilts
For daggers in plaid socks; of smart salutes;
And care of arms; and leave; and pay arrears;
*Esprit de corps*; and hints for young recruits.
And soon he was drafted out with drums and cheers.

. . . . . .

Some cheered him home, but not as crowds cheer Goal.
Only a solemn man who brought him fruits
*Thanked* him; and then inquired about his soul.

. . . . .

Now, he will spend a few sick years in Institutes,
And do what things the rules consider wise,
And take whatever pity they may dole.
To-night he noticed how the women's eyes
Passed from him to the strong men that were whole.
How cold and late it is! Why don't they come
And put him into bed? Why don't they come?

# SONNET

Be slowly lifted up, thou long black arm,
Great gun towering toward Heaven, about to curse;
Sway steep against them, and for years rehearse
Huge imprecations like a blasting charm!
Reach at that arrogance which needs thy harm,
And beat it down before its sins grow worse;
Spend our resentment, cannon, yea, disburse
Our gold in shapes of flame, our breaths in storm.

Yet, for men's sakes whom thy vast malison
Must wither innocent of enmity,
Be not withdrawn, dark arm, thy spoilure done,
Safe to the bosom of our prosperity.
But when thy spell be cast complete and whole,
May God curse thee, and cut thee from our soul!

# SONNET

**TO A CHILD**

Sweet is your antique body, not yet young;
Beauty withheld from youth that looks for youth;
Fair only for your father. Dear among
Masters in art. To all men else uncouth;
Save me, who know your smile comes very old,
Learnt of the happy dead that laughed with gods;
For earlier suns than ours have lent you gold;
Sly fauns and trees have given you jigs and nods.

But soon your heart, hot-beating like a bird's,
Shall slow down. Youth shall lop your hair;
And you must learn wry meanings in our words.
Your smile shall dull, because too keen aware;
And when for hopes your hand shall be uncurled,
Your eyes shall close, being open to the world.

# THE FATES

They watch me, those informers to the Fates,
Called Fortune, Chance, Necessity, and Death;
Time, in disguise as one who serves and waits,
Eternity, as girls of fragrant breath.
I know them. Men and boys are in their pay,
And those I hold my trustiest friends may prove
Agents of Theirs to take me if I stray
From fatal ordinance. If I move they move—

Escape? There is one unwatched way: your eyes,
O Beauty! Keep me good that secret gate.
And when the cordon tightens of the spies
Let the close iris of your eyes grow great.
So I'll evade the vice and rack of age
And miss the march of lifetime, stage by stage.

*June 2*, 1917.

# ANTHEM FOR DOOMED YOUTH

What passing-bells for these who die as cattle?
  Only the monstrous anger of the guns.
  Only the stuttering rifles' rapid rattle
Can patter out their hasty orisons.
No mockeries for them from prayers or bells,
  Nor any voice of mourning save the choirs,—
The shrill, demented choirs of wailing shells;
  And bugles calling for them from sad shires.

What candles may be held to speed them all?
  Not in the hands of boys, but in their eyes
Shall shine the holy glimmers of good-byes.
  The pallor of girls' brows shall be their pall;
Their flowers the tenderness of silent minds,
And each slow dusk a drawing-down of blinds.

# THE NEXT WAR

War's a joke for me and you,
While we know such dreams are true.
                                    SASSOON.

Out there, we've walked quite friendly up to Death;
    Sat down and eaten with him, cool and bland,—
    Pardoned his spilling mess-tins in our hand.
We've sniffed the green thick odour of his breath,—
Our eyes wept, but our courage didn't writhe.
    He's spat at us with bullets and he's coughed
    Shrapnel. We chorussed when he sang aloft;
We whistled while he shaved us with his scythe.

Oh, Death was never enemy of ours!
    We laughed at him, we leagued with him, old chum.
No soldier's paid to kick against his powers.
    We laughed, knowing that better men would come,
And greater wars; when each proud fighter brags
He wars on Death—for Life; not men—for flags.

# SONG OF SONGS

Sing me at morn but only with your laugh;
Even as Spring that laugheth into leaf;
Even as Love that laugheth after Life.

Sing me but only with your speech all day,
As voluble leaflets do; let viols die;
The least word of your lips is melody!

Sing me at eve but only with your sigh!
Like lifting seas it solaceth; breathe so,
Slowly and low, the sense that no songs say.

Sing me at midnight with your murmurous heart!
Let youth's immortal-moaning chords be heard
Throbbing through you, and sobbing, unsubdued.

# ALL SOUNDS HAVE BEEN AS MUSIC

All sounds have been as music to my listening:
   Pacific lamentations of slow bells,
The crunch of boots on blue snow rosy-glistening,
   Shuffle of autumn leaves; and all farewells:

Bugles that sadden all the evening air,
   And country bells clamouring their last appeals
Before [the] music of the evening prayer;
   Bridges, sonorous under carriage wheels.

Gurgle of sluicing surge through hollow rocks,
   The gluttonous lapping of the waves on weeds,
Whisper of grasses; the myriad-tinkling flocks,
   The warbling drawl of flutes and shepherds' reeds.

The orchestral noises of October nights
   Blowing [                    ] symphonetic storms
Of startled clarions [                        ]
   Drums, rumbling and rolling thunderous and [   ].

Thrilling of throstles in the clear blue dawn,
   Bees fumbling and fuming over sainfoin-fields.

   .     .     .     .     .     .

# VOICES

Bugles sang, saddening the evening air,
And bugles answered, sorrowful to hear.

Voices of boys were by the river-side.
Sleep mothered them; and left the twilight sad.
The shadow of the morrow weighed on men.

Voices of old despondency resigned,
Bowed by the shadow of the morrow, slept.

[                           ] dying tone
Of receding voices that will not return.
The wailing of the high far-travelling shells
And the deep cursing of the provoking [     ].

The monstrous anger of our taciturn guns.
The majesty of the insults of their mouths.

# APOLOGIA PRO POEMATE MEO

I, too, saw God through mud,—
    The mud that cracked on cheeks when wretches smiled.
    War brought more glory to their eyes than blood,
    And gave their laughs more glee than shakes a child.

Merry it was to laugh there—
    Where death becomes absurd and life absurder.
    For power was on us as we slashed bones bare
    Not to feel sickness or remorse of murder.

I, too, have dropped off fear—
    Behind the barrage, dead as my platoon,
    And sailed my spirit surging, light and clear
    Past the entanglement where hopes lay strewn;

And witnessed exultation—
    Faces that used to curse me, scowl for scowl,
    Shine and lift up with passion of oblation,
    Seraphic for an hour; though they were foul.

I have made fellowships—
    Untold of happy lovers in old song.
    For love is not the binding of fair lips
    With the soft silk of eyes that look and long,

By Joy, whose ribbon slips,—
    But wound with war's hard wire whose stakes are strong;
    Bound with the bandage of the arm that drips;
    Knit in the webbing of the rifle-thong.

I have perceived much beauty
    In the hoarse oaths that kept our courage straight;

Heard music in the silentness of duty;
Found peace where shell-storms spouted reddest spate.

Nevertheless, except you share
With them in hell the sorrowful dark of hell,
Whose world is but the trembling of a flare,
And heaven but as the highway for a shell,

You shall not hear their mirth:
You shall not come to think them well content
By any jest of mine. These men are worth
Your tears. You are not worth their merriment.

*November* 1917.

# À TERRE

### (BEING THE PHILOSOPHY OF MANY SOLDIERS)

Sit on the bed. I'm blind, and three parts shell.
Be careful; can't shake hands now; never shall.
Both arms have mutinied against me,—brutes.
My fingers fidget like ten idle brats.

I tried to peg out soldierly,—no use!
One dies of war like any old disease.
This bandage feels like pennies on my eyes.
I have my medals?—Discs to make eyes close.
My glorious ribbons?—Ripped from my own back
In scarlet shreds. (That's for your poetry book.)

A short life and a merry one, my buck!
We used to say we'd hate to live dead-old,—
Yet now . . . I'd willingly be puffy, bald,
And patriotic. Buffers catch from boys
At least the jokes hurled at them. I suppose
Little I'd ever teach a son, but hitting,
Shooting, war, hunting, all the arts of hurting.
Well, that's what I learnt,—that, and making money.

Your fifty years ahead seem none too many?
Tell me how long I've got? God! For one year
To help myself to nothing more than air!
One Spring! Is one too good to spare, too long?
Spring wind would work its own way to my lung,
And grow me legs as quick as lilac-shoots.

My servant's lamed, but listen how he shouts!
When I'm lugged out, he'll still be good for that.

Here in this mummy-case, you know, I've thought
How well I might have swept his floors for ever.
I'd ask no nights off when the bustle's over,
Enjoying so the dirt. Who's prejudiced
Against a grimed hand when his own's quite dust,
Less live than specks that in the sun-shafts turn,
Less warm than dust that mixes with arms' tan?
I'd love to be a sweep, now, black as Town,
Yes; or a muckman. Must I be his load?

O Life, Life, let me breathe,—a dug-out rat!
Not worse than ours the existences rats lead—
Nosing along at night down some safe rut,
They find a shell-proof home before they rot.
Dead men may envy living mites in cheese,
Or good germs even. Microbes have their joys,
And subdivide, and never come to death.
Certainly flowers have the easiest time on earth.
"I shall be one with nature, herb, and stone",
Shelley would tell me. Shelley would be stunned:
The dullest Tommy hugs that fancy now.
"Pushing up daisies" is their creed, you know.
To grain, then, go my fat, to buds my sap,
For all the usefulness there is in soap.
D'you think the Boche will ever stew man-soup?
Some day, no doubt, if . . .

                    Friend, be very sure
I shall be better off with plants that share
More peaceably the meadow and the shower.
Soft rains will touch me,—as they could touch once,
And nothing but the sun shall make me ware.
Your guns may crash around me. I'll not hear;
Or, if I wince, I shall not know I wince.
Don't take my soul's poor comfort for your jest.
Soldiers may grow a soul when turned to fronds,
But here the thing's best left at home with friends.

My soul's a little grief, grappling your chest,
To climb your throat on sobs; easily chased
On other sighs and wiped by fresher winds.

Carry my crying spirit till it's weaned
To do without what blood remained these wounds.

# WILD WITH ALL REGRETS

## (ANOTHER VERSION OF "À TERRE")

### *To Siegfried Sassoon*


My arms have mutinied against me,—brutes!
My fingers fidget like ten idle brats,
My back's been stiff for hours, damned hours.
Death never gives his squad a Stand-at-ease.
I can't read. There: it's no use. Take your book.
A short life and a merry one, my buck!
We said we'd hate to grow dead-old. But now,
Not to live old seems awful: not to renew
My boyhood with my boys, and teach 'em hitting,
Shooting, and hunting,—all the arts of hurting!
—Well, that's what I learnt. That, and making money.
Your fifty years in store seem none too many,
But I've five minutes. God! For just two years
To help myself to this good air of yours!
One Spring! Is one too hard to spare? Too long?
Spring air would find its own way to my lung,
And grow me legs as quick as lilac-shoots.

  .  .  .  .  .  .

Yes, there's the orderly. He'll change the sheets
When I'm lugged out. Oh, couldn't I do that?
Here in this coffin of a bed, I've thought
I'd like to kneel and sweep his floors for ever,—
And ask no nights off when the bustle's over,
For I'd enjoy the dirt. Who's prejudiced
Against a grimed hand when his own's quite dust,—
Less live than specks that in the sun-shafts turn?
Dear dust—in rooms, on roads, on faces' tan!

I'd love to be a sweep's boy, black as Town;
Yes, or a muckman. Must I be his load?
A flea would do. If one chap wasn't bloody,
Or went stone-cold, I'd find another body.

    .     .     .     .     .     .

Which I shan't manage now. Unless it's yours.
I shall stay in you, friend, for some few hours.
You'll feel my heavy spirit chill your chest,
And climb your throat on sobs, until it's chased
On sighs, and wiped from off your lips by wind.

I think on your rich breathing, brother, I'll be weaned
To do without what blood remained me from my wound.

*December* 5, 1917.

# WINTER SONG

The browns, the olives, and the yellows died,
And were swept up to heaven; where they glowed
Each dawn and set of sun till Christmastide,
And when the land lay pale for them, pale-snowed,
Fell back, and down the snow-drifts flamed and flowed.

From off your face, into the winds of winter,
The sun-brown and the summer-gold are blowing;
But they shall gleam [again] with spiritual glinter,
When paler beauty on your brows falls snowing,
And through those snows my looks shall be soft-going.

*October* 18, 1917.

# HOSPITAL BARGE AT CÉRISY

Budging the sluggard ripples of the Somme,
A barge round old Cérisy slowly slewed.
Softly her engines down the current screwed
And chuckled in her, with contented hum.
Till fairy tinklings struck their crooning dumb,
And waters rumpling at the stern subdued.
The lock-gate took her bulging amplitude.
Gently into the gurgling lock she swum.

One reading by that sunset raised his eyes
To watch her lessening westward quietly;
Till, as she neared the bend, her funnel screamed.
And that long lamentation made him wise
How unto Avalon in agony
Kings passed in the dark barge which Merlin dreamed.

*December* 8, 1917.

# SIX O'CLOCK IN PRINCES STREET

In twos and threes, they have not far to roam,
    Crowds that thread eastward, gay of eyes;
Those seek no further than their quiet home,
    Wives, walking westward, slow and wise.

Neither should I go fooling over clouds,
    Following gleams unsafe, untrue,
And tiring after beauty through star-crowds,
    Dared I go side by side with you;

Or be you on the gutter where you stand,
    Pale rain-flawed phantom of the place,
With news of all the nations in your hand,
    And all their sorrows in your face.

# THE ROADS ALSO

The roads also have their wistful rest,
When the weathercocks perch still and roost,
And the town is [quiet like] a candle-lit room—
The streets also dream their dream.

The old houses muse of the old days
And their fond trees leaning on them doze,
On their steps chatter and clatter stops,
On their doors a strange hand taps.

Men remember alien [          ] ardours
As the dusk unearths old mournful odours.
In the garden unborn child souls wail
And the dead scribble on walls.

Though their own child cry for them in tears,
Women weep but hear no sound upstairs.
They believe in loves they had not lived
And in passion past the reach of the stairs
        To the world's towers or stars.

# THIS IS THE TRACK

This is the track my life is setting on,
    Spacious the spanless way I wend;
The blackness of darkness may be held for me?
    And barren plunging without end?

Why dare I fear? For other wandering souls
    Burn thro' the night of that far bourne.
And they are light unto themselves; and aureoles
    Self-radiated there are worn.

And when in after-times we make return
    Round solar bounds awhile to run,
They gather many satellites astern
    And turn aside the very sun.

# THE CALLS

A dismal fog-hoarse siren howls at dawn.
I watch the man it calls for, pushed and drawn
Backwards and forwards, helpless as a pawn.
       But I'm lazy, and his work's crazy.

Quick treble bells begin at nine o'clock,
Scuttling the schoolboy pulling up his sock,
Scaring the late girl in the inky frock.
       I must be crazy; I learn from the daisy.

Stern bells annoy the rooks and doves at ten.
I watch the verger close the doors, and when
I hear the organ moan the first amen,
       Sing my religions—same as pigeons.

A blatant bugle tears my afternoons.
Out clump the clumsy Tommies by platoons,
Trying to keep in step with rag-time tunes,
       But I sit still; I've done my drill.

# MINERS

There was a whispering in my hearth,
    A sigh of the coal,
Grown wistful of a former earth
    It might recall.

I listened for a tale of leaves
    And smothered ferns;
Frond-forests; and the low, sly lives
    Before the fawns.

My fire might show steam-phantoms simmer
    From Time's old cauldron,
Before the birds made nests in summer,
    Or men had children.

But the coals were murmuring of their mine,
    And moans down there
Of boys that slept wry sleep, and men
    Writhing for air.

And I saw white bones in the cinder-shard.
    Bones without number;
For many hearts with coal are charred
    And few remember.

I thought of some who worked dark pits
    Of war, and died
Digging the rock where Death reputes
    Peace lies indeed.

Comforted years will sit soft-chaired
    In rooms of amber;

The years will stretch their hands, well-cheered
 By our lives' ember.

The centuries will burn rich loads
 With which we groaned,
Whose warmth shall lull their dreaming lids
 While songs are crooned.
But they will not dream of us poor lads
 Lost in the ground.

# AND I MUST GO

Gongs hum and buzz like saucepan-lid at dusk,
I see a food-hog whet his gold-filled tusk
To eat less bread, and more luxurious rusk.

Then sometimes late at night my window bumps
From gunnery-practice, till my small heart thumps
And listens for the shell-shrieks and the crumps,
        But that's not all.

For leaning out last midnight on my sill
I heard the sighs of men, that have no skill
To speak of their distress, no, nor the will!
        A voice I know. And I must go.

# THE PROMISERS

When I awoke, the glancing day looked gay;
The air said: Fare you fleetly; you will meet him!
And when the prosp'rous sun was well begun,
I heard a bird say: Sweetly you shall greet him!

The sun felt strong and bold upon my shoulder;
It hung, it clung as it were my friend's arm.
The birds fifed on before, shrill-piping pipers,
Right down to town; and there they ceased to charm.

And there I wandered till the noon came soon,
And chimed: The time is hastening with his face!
Sly twilight said: I bring him; wait till late!
But darkness harked forlorn to my lone pace.

# TRAINING

Not this week nor this month dare I lie down
In languor under lime trees or [smooth smile].
Love must not kiss my face pale that is brown.

My lips, parting, shall drink space, mile by mile;
Strong meats be all my hunger; my renown
Be the clean beauty of speed and pride of style.

Cold winds encountered on the racing Down
Shall thrill my heated bareness; but awhile
None else may meet me till I wear my Crown.

*June* 1918.

# THE KIND GHOSTS

She sleeps on soft, last breaths; but no ghost looms
Out of the stillness of her palace wall,
Her wall of boys on boys and dooms on dooms.

She dreams of golden gardens and sweet glooms,
Not marvelling why her roses never fall
Nor what red mouths were torn to make their blooms.

The shades keep down which well might roam her hall.
Quiet their blood lies in her crimson rooms
And she is not afraid of their footfall.

They move not from her tapestries, their pall,
Nor pace her terraces, their hecatombs,
Lest aught she be disturbed, or grieved at all.

# TO MY FRIEND

## (WITH AN IDENTITY DISC)

If ever I had dreamed of my dead name
  High in the heart of London, unsurpassed
By Time for ever, and the Fugitive, Fame,
  There seeking a long sanctuary at last,—

Or if I onetime hoped to hide its shame,
—Shame of success, and sorrow of defeats,—
Under those holy cypresses, the same
  That shade always the quiet place of Keats,

Now rather thank I God there is no risk
  Of gravers scoring it with florid screed.
Let my inscription be this soldier's disc. . . .
  Wear it, sweet friend, inscribe no date nor deed.
But may thy heart-beat kiss it, night and day,
Until the name grow blurred and fade away.

1918.

# INSPECTION

"You! What d'you mean by this?" I rapped.
"You dare come on parade like this?"
"Please, sir, it's——"  " 'Old yer mouth," the sergeant
    snapped.
"I take 'is name, sir?"—"Please, and then dismiss."

Some days "confined to camp" he got
For being "dirty on parade".
He told me afterwards, the damned spot
Was blood, his own. "Well, blood is dirt," I said.

"Blood's dirt," he laughed, looking away
Far off to where his wound had bled
And almost merged for ever into clay.
"The world is washing out its stains," he said.
"It doesn't like our cheeks so red.
Young blood's its great objection.
But when we're duly white-washed, being dead,
The race will bear Field-Marshal God's inspection."

# FRAGMENT: A FAREWELL

I saw his round mouth's crimson deepen as it fell,
    Like a Sun, in his last deep hour;
Watched the magnificent recession of farewell,
    Clouding, half gleam, half glower,
And a last splendour burn the heavens of his cheek.
    And in his eyes
The cold stars lighting, very old and bleak,
    In different skies.

# FRAGMENT: THE ABYSS OF WAR

As bronze may be much beautified
By lying in the dark damp soil,
So men who fade in dust of warfare fade
Fairer, and sorrow blooms their soul.

Like pearls which noble women wear
And, tarnishing, awhile confide
Unto the old salt sea to feed,
Many return more lustrous than they were.

But what of them buried profound,
Buried where we can no more find,
Who [                                    ]
Lie dark for ever under abysmal war?

# AT A CALVARY NEAR THE ANCRE

One ever hangs where shelled roads part.
  In this war He too lost a limb,
But His disciples hide apart;
  And now the Soldiers bear with Him.

Near Golgotha strolls many a priest,
  And in their faces there is pride
That they were flesh-marked by the Beast
  By whom the gentle Christ's denied.

The scribes on all the people shove
  And bawl allegiance to the state,
But they who love the greater love
  Lay down their life; they do not hate.

# LE CHRISTIANISME

So the church Christ was hit and buried
   Under its rubbish and its rubble.
In cellars, packed-up saints lie serried,
   Well out of hearing of our trouble.

One Virgin still immaculate
   Smiles on for war to flatter her.
She's halo'd with an old tin hat,
   But a piece of hell will batter her.

QUIVIÈRES.

# SPRING OFFENSIVE

Halted against the shade of a last hill,
They fed, and, lying easy, were at ease
And, finding comfortable chests and knees,
Carelessly slept. But many there stood still
To face the stark, blank sky beyond the ridge,
Knowing their feet had come to the end of the world.

Marvelling they stood, and watched the long grass swirled
By the May breeze, murmurous with wasp and midge,
For though the summer oozed into their veins
Like an injected drug for their bodies' pains,
Sharp on their souls hung the imminent line of grass,
Fearfully flashed the sky's mysterious glass.

Hour after hour they ponder the warm field—
And the far valley behind, where the buttercup
Had blessed with gold their slow boots coming up,
Where even the little brambles would not yield,
But clutched and clung to them like sorrowing hands;
They breathe like trees unstirred.

Till like a cold gust thrills the little word
At which each body and its soul begird
And tighten them for battle. No alarms
Of bugles, no high flags, no clamorous haste—
Only a lift and flare of eyes that faced
The sun, like a friend with whom their love is done.
O larger shone that smile against the sun,—
Mightier than his whose bounty these have spurned.

So, soon they topped the hill, and raced together
Over an open stretch of herb and heather

Exposed. And instantly the whole sky burned
With fury against them; earth set sudden cups
In thousands for their blood; and the green slope
Chasmed and steepened sheer to infinite space.

. . . . . .

Of them who running on that last high place
Leapt to swift unseen bullets, or went up
On the hot blast and fury of hell's upsurge,
Or plunged and fell away past this world's verge,
Some say God caught them even before they fell.

But what say such as from existence' brink
Ventured but drave too swift to sink,
The few who rushed in the body to enter hell,
And there out-fiending all its fiends and flames
With superhuman inhumanities,
Long-famous glories, immemorial shames—
And crawling slowly back, have by degrees
Regained cool peaceful air in wonder—
Why speak not they of comrades that went under?

# THE SENTRY

We'd found an old Boche dug-out, and he knew,
And gave us hell, for shell on frantic shell
Hammered on top, but never quite burst through.
Rain, guttering down in waterfalls of slime
Kept slush waist-high that, rising hour by hour,
Choked up the steps too thick with clay to climb.
What murk of air remained stank old, and sour
With fumes of whizz-bangs, and the smell of men
Who'd lived there years, and left their curse in the den,
If not their corpses. . . .
                There we herded from the blast
Of whizz-bangs, but one found our door at last,—
Buffeting eyes and breath, snuffing the candles.
And thud! flump! thud! down the steep steps came
    thumping
And splashing in the flood, deluging muck—
The sentry's body; then, his rifle, handles
Of old Boche bombs, and mud in ruck on ruck.
We dredged him up, for killed, until he whined
"O sir, my eyes—I'm blind—I'm blind, I'm blind!"
Coaxing, I held a flame against his lids
And said if he could see the least blurred light
He was not blind; in time he'd get all right.
"I can't," he sobbed. Eyeballs, huge-bulged like squids',
Watch my dreams still; but I forgot him there
In posting next for duty, and sending a scout
To beg a stretcher somewhere, and floundering about
To other posts under the shrieking air.

Those other wretches, how they bled and spewed,
And one who would have drowned himself for good,—
I try not to remember these things now.

Let dread hark back for one word only: how
Half listening to that sentry's moans and jumps,
And the wild chattering of his broken teeth,
Renewed most horribly whenever crumps
Pummelled the roof and slogged the air beneath—
Through the dense din, I say, we heard him shout
"I see your lights!" But ours had long died out.

# SMILE, SMILE, SMILE

Head to limp head, the sunk-eyed wounded scanned
Yesterday's *Mail*; the casualties (typed small)
And (large) Vast Booty from our Latest Haul.
Also, they read of Cheap Homes, not yet planned
For, said the paper, "When this war is done
The men's first instinct will be making homes.
Meanwhile their foremost need is aerodromes,
It being certain war has but begun.
Peace would do wrong to our undying dead,—
The sons we offered might regret they died
If we got nothing lasting in their stead.
We must be solidly indemnified.
Though all be worthy Victory which all bought,
We rulers sitting in this ancient spot
Would wrong our very selves if we forgot
The greatest glory will be theirs who fought,
Who kept this nation in integrity."
Nation?—The half-limbed readers did not chafe
But smiled at one another curiously
Like secret men who know their secret safe.
(This is the thing they know and never speak,
That England one by one had fled to France,
Not many elsewhere now save under France.)
Pictures of these broad smiles appear each week,
And people in whose voice real feeling rings
Say: How they smile! They're happy now, poor things.

*23rd September* 1918.

# THE END

After the blast of lightning from the East,
The flourish of loud clouds, the Chariot Throne;
After the drums of Time have rolled and ceased,
And by the bronze west long retreat is blown,

Shall life renew these bodies? Of a truth
All death will He annul, all tears assuage?—
Fill the void veins of Life again with youth,
And wash, with an immortal water, Age?

When I do ask white Age he saith not so:
"My head hangs weighed with snow."
And when I hearken to the Earth, she saith:
"My fiery heart shrinks, aching. It is death.
Mine ancient scars shall not be glorified,
Nor my titanic tears, the sea, be dried."

# STRANGE MEETING

It seemed that out of battle I escaped
Down some profound dull tunnel, long since scooped
Through granites which titanic wars had groined.
Yet also there encumbered sleepers groaned,
Too fast in thought or death to be bestirred.
Then, as I probed them, one sprang up, and stared
With piteous recognition in fixed eyes,
Lifting distressful hands as if to bless.
And by his smile, I knew that sullen hall,
By his dead smile I knew we stood in Hell.
With a thousand pains that vision's face was grained;
Yet no blood reached there from the upper ground,
And no guns thumped, or down the flues made moan.
"Strange friend," I said, "here is no cause to mourn."
"None," said the other, "save the undone years,
The hopelessness. Whatever hope is yours,
Was my life also; I went hunting wild
After the wildest beauty in the world,
Which lies not calm in eyes, or braided hair,
But mocks the steady running of the hour,
And if it grieves, grieves richlier than here.
For by my glee might many men have laughed,
And of my weeping something had been left,
Which must die now. I mean the truth untold,
The pity of war, the pity war distilled.
Now men will go content with what we spoiled.
Or, discontent, boil bloody, and be spilled.
They will be swift with swiftness of the tigress,
None will break ranks, though nations trek from progress.
Courage was mine, and I had mystery,
Wisdom was mine, and I had mastery;
To miss the march of this retreating world

Into vain citadels that are not walled.
Then, when much blood had clogged their chariot-wheels
I would go up and wash them from sweet wells,
Even with truths that lie too deep for taint.
I would have poured my spirit without stint
But not through wounds; not on the cess of war.
Foreheads of men have bled where no wounds were.
I am the enemy you killed, my friend.
I knew you in this dark; for so you frowned
Yesterday through me as you jabbed and killed.
I parried; but my hands were loath and cold.
Let us sleep now. . . ."

# DISTRIBUTORS
*for the Wordsworth Poetry Library*

**AUSTRALIA, BRUNEI,
MALAYSIA & SINGAPORE**

Reed Editions
22 Salmon Street
Port Melbourne
Vic 3207
Australia

Tel: (03) 646 6716
Fax: (03) 646 6925

**GREAT BRITAIN & IRELAND**

Wordsworth Editions Ltd
Cumberland House
Crib Street
Ware
Hertfordshire SG12 9ET

**HOLLAND & BELGIUM**

Uitgeverij en Boekhandel
Van Gennup BV, Spuistraat 283
1012 VR Amsterdam, Holland

**INDIA**

Om Book Service
1690 First Floor
Nai Sarak, Delhi - 110006

Tel: 3279823/3265303
Fax: 3278091

**ITALY**

Magis Books
Piazza della Vittoria 1/C
42100 Reggio Emilia

Tel: 0522-452303
Fax: 0522-452845

**NEW ZEALAND**

Whitcoulls Limited
Private Bag 92098, Auckland

**SOUTH AFRICA, ZIMBABWE
CENTRAL & E AFRICA**

Trade Winds Press (Pty) Ltd
PO Box 20194, Durban North 4016

**USA, CANADA & MEXICO**

Universal Sales & Marketing
230 Fifth Avenue
Suite 1212
New York, NY 10001 USA

Tel: 212-481-3500
Fax: 212-481-3534